Football's
FUNNIEST
QUOTES!

Harry Kaye

Thanks

We couldn't have put this book together without the wonderful characters in the world of football. They truly do come up with some fantastic nonsense – some intentional but much of it unintentional.

When you're commentating live to millions of people, or having a microphone thrust in your face minutes after a game, it's no surprise that sometimes your words don't come out quite as planned... and for that we're very grateful. So, we do hope you enjoy laughing along with the true stars quoted in this book.

The Quotes

You can't argue with that logic

Most goals are scored between the posts.

JAMIE REDKNAPP

We need to stop conceding and score more.

DAVID MOYES

Bayern will have the added advantage of playing in their own stadium. That's like a home game for them.

PAUL ELLIOTT

I don't want Rooney to leave these shores but if he does, I think he'll go abroad.

IAN WRIGHT

I think goals are important this season.

GARY MCALLISTER

If you make the right decision, it's normally going to be the correct one.

DAVE BASSETT

I was a young lad when I was growing up.

DAVID O'LEARY

I'm a firm believer that if the other side scores first you have to score twice to win.

HOWARD WILKINSON

It's interesting that the games in which we've dropped points are those where we've failed to score.

SIR ALEX FERGUSON

I've seen players sent off for worse than that.

JOE ROYLE

It's very important to win the must-win games.

MARTIN KEOWN

If I was still at Ipswich, I wouldn't be where I am today.

DALIAN ATKINSON

The interesting thing about Nani is that he has two feet.

RAY WILKINS

So this movie you star in, 'The Life Story Of George Best', tell us what it's about.

GEORGE GAVIN

Sometimes in football you have to score goals.

THIERRY HENRY

Sometimes it's better to be lucky than unlucky.

GLENN HODDLE

I've always been a childhood Liverpool fan, even when I was a kid.

HARRY KEWELL

Leeds are enjoying more possession now that they have the ball.

SIMON BROTHERTON

Merseyside derbies usually last 90 minutes and I'm sure today's won't be any different.

TREVOR BROOKING

The area you're trying to protect at corners is the goal.

CHRIS KAMARA

When they don't score they hardly ever win.

MICHAEL OWEN

Not only has he shown Junior Lewis the red card, but he's sent him off!

CHRIS KAMARA

When you don't score goals it is not easy to win.
JUANDE RAMOS

When you score one goal more than the other team in a cup tie it is always enough.
CESARE MALDINI

What can I say about Peter Shilton? Peter Shilton is Peter Shilton, and he has been Peter Shilton since the year dot.
SIR BOBBY ROBSON

West Brom have won a few late points. Do those points help or hinder them? I think they help them.
PHIL THOMPSON

That's exactly how you head a ball. You use your head.

RAY WILKINS

The substitute is about to come on - he's a player who was left out of the starting line-up today.

KEVIN KEEGAN

Walsall have given City more than one anxious moment amongst many anxious moments.

DENIS LAW

We are really quite lucky this year because Christmas falls on Christmas Day.

BOBBY GOULD

Well, either side could win it, or it could be a draw.

RON ATKINSON

There was nothing between us and United ...
apart from the seven goals.

DANNY WILSON

There's only one moment in which you can
arrive in time. If you're not there, you're either
too early or too late.

JOHAN CRUYFF

They only count when they go in the goal.

CHRIS KAMARA

They were numerically outnumbered.

GARRY BIRTLES

What I saw in Holland and Germany was that
the majority of people are Dutch in Holland and
German in Germany.

PETER TAYLOR

They've flown in from all over the world, have the rest of the world team.

BRIAN MOORE

You have got to shoot, otherwise you can't score.

JOHAN CRUYFF

You have to finish above everyone to win the league.

ROY EVANS

Your chest is different to your head.

GLENN HODDLE

It's Ipswich 0 Liverpool 2, and if that's the way the score stays then you've got to fancy Liverpool to win.

PETER JONES

You can never compare two players that are different. They're never going to be the same.

GLENN HODDLE

I read Michael Caine's biography. It was about him growing up.

FRANK LAMPARD

Leeds have only had one shot on target, which may well have been the goal.

ANDY GRAY

The only way to beat Liverpool is to score more goals than them.

STEVE CLARIDGE

The unthinkable is not something we are thinking about at the moment.

PETER KENYON

We're moving up the table now which is hopefully the right direction.

PAUL ROBINSON

The Brazilians were South American, and the Ukranians will be more European.

PHIL NEAL

When you are 4-0 up you should never lose 7-1.

LAWRIE MCMENEMY

Are you joking?!

It's like a toaster, the ref's shirt pocket. Every time there's a tackle, up pops a yellow card.

KEVIN KEEGAN

[Ken] Bates always had to be one up on you. If you told him you'd been to Tenerife, he'd say he'd been to Elevenerife.

DAVID SPEEDIE

He can't remember too much about what happened. He came over to the bench and said he wanted to carry on, so we told him he was Pele.

GLENN HODDLE ON LES FERDINAND

He's still young, but he's getting older every year.

DARREN GOUGH ON MARIO BALOTELLI

I believe a young man will run through a barbed-wire fence for you. An older player looks for a hole in the fence.

BRENDAN RODGERS

I just wanted to give them some technical advice. I told them the game had started.

RON ATKINSON

I told him Newcastle was nearer to London than Middlesbrough, and he believed me.

KEVIN KEEGAN

I told my players during the break: Since we're here anyway, we might actually play a bit of football.

JURGEN KLOPP

You can see the ball go past them, or the man, but you'll never see both man and ball go past at the same time. So if the ball goes past, the man wont, or if the man goes past they'll take the ball.

RON ATKINSON

In the first half we were like the Dog And Duck.
In the second half we were like Real Madrid.
We can't go on like that. At full time I was at
them like an irritated Jack Russell.

IAN HOLLOWAY

Well Tim, I guess my advice to you would be
this: make as many saves as you can.
KASEY KELLER'S ADVICE FOR TIM HOWARD

It's like trying to push custard up a hill!
HOWARD WILKINSON

Manchester City are defending like beavers.
CHRIS KAMARA

When I score, I don't celebrate because it's my
job. When a postman delivers letters, does he
celebrate?
MARIO BALOTELLI

So, Gordon, in what areas do you think
Middlesbrough were better than you today? -
What areas? Mainly that big green one out
there...

GORDON STRACHAN

The Liverpool players are passing the cup down
the line like a new born baby. Although when
they are back in the dressing room they will
probably fill it with champagne, something you
should never do to a baby.

ALAN PARRY

We had a good team on paper. Unfortunately,
the game was played on grass.

BRIAN CLOUGH

The Sheffield United board have been loyal to
me. When I came here they said there would be
no money and they've kept their promise.

DAVE BASSETT

Up front we played like world beaters – at the back it was more like panel beaters.

PAUL JEWELL

Thierry Henry was literally like a fish up a tree.
LEE DIXON

Young players are a little bit like melons. Only when you open and taste the melon are you 100 per cent sure that the melon is good. Sometimes you have beautiful melons but they don't taste very good and some other melons are a bit ugly and when you open them, the taste is fantastic... One thing is youth football, one thing is professional football. The bridge is a difficult one to cross and they have to play with us and train with us for us to taste the melon.
JOSE MOURINHO

We're not used to weather in June in this country.
JIMMY HILL

We were caviar in the first half, cabbage in the second.

PHIL THOMPSON

We've had Jack Marriott score for Luton and Danny Hylton has scored for Oxford United. We just need Tommy Travelodge to score for a unique hat trick.

JEFF STELLING

When you finish playing football, young man, which is going to be very soon, I feel, you'll make a very good security guard.

DAVID PLEAT TO A 17-YEAR OLD NEIL RUDDOCK

When you speak to Barry Fry, it's like completing a 1,000-piece jigsaw.

BRIAN MOORE

What is Brexit? I think it's a dance. I may be wrong.

NOLITO

When I first started getting called Champagne Charlie. I couldn't afford champagne! I was on the shandy, if I was lucky.

CHARLIE NICHOLAS

When I say that he needs to stand up and be counted, I mean that he needs to sit down and take a look at himself in the mirror.

GARY MABBUTT'S

When Rioch came to Millwall we were depressed and miserable. He's done a brilliant job of turning it all around. Now we're miserable and depressed.

DANNY BAKER

When I went to Liverpool, I must admit it was more of a culture shock than coming to France.

JOE COLE

Erik Thorstvedt said Spurs had sold Elvis and bought the Beatles; but a Norwegian would.

JEFF STELLING

For me, pressure is bird flu. I'm feeling a lot of pressure with the problem in Scotland. It's not fun and I'm more scared of it than football.

JOSE MOURINHO

Being at United was a culture shock for me. Even the loos had gold taps.

GARY BIRTLES

You cant do better than go away from home and get a draw.

KEVIN KEEGAN

Will I become a coach in the future? No way. I'd never be able to put up with someone like me.

ROMARIO

With all those replica strips in the stands, coming to Newcastle is like playing in front of 40,000 baying zebras.

DAVID PLEAT

You may as well put a cow in the middle of the pitch, walking. And then stop the game because there was a cow.

JOSE MOURINHO ON TIME WASTING

Bridge has done nothing wrong, but his movement's not great and his distribution's been poor.

ALAN MULLERY

Arsene Wenger wrote a nice card and Alex
Ferguson said he wanted to see me back in the
dugout soon and told me to back one of his
horses at Cheltenham. I did and it came fourth.
Thanks Alex, just what I needed to relax!

JOE KINNEAR AFTER A HEART OPERATION

At Newcastle I was older than the manager,
older than the assistant manager, older than the
physio and the club doctor – which must be
some sort of record.

STUART PEARCE

At the end of today's third round, players you've
never heard of will be household names – like
that fellow who scored for Sutton United against
Coventry last season.

BOBBY CAMPBELL

Time for some inspiration

Being a goalkeeper is like being the guy
in the military who makes the bombs -
one mistake and everyone gets blown up.

ARTUR BORUC

I'm very proud, I'm super proud, I'm the proudest man in Proudsville.

SEAN DYCHE

When your own fans whistle and jeer, then you have a big problem.

ZINEDINE ZIDANE

There is definitely a price to pay. The biggest thing I miss because of football is that I really, really love to go on a skiing holiday but as long as I have my career, I can't do that because of the risk of being injured.

NICKLAS BENDTNER

Management is the only job in the world where everyone knows better. I would never tell a plumber, a lawyer or a journalist how to do his job but they all know better than me every Saturday.

JOE ROYLE

You shouldn't be nuts, but it doesn't matter if you are a bit peculiar.

PETER SCHMEICHEL

Why am I the best in the world? Because I am, that's all.

CLAUDE MAKELELE

Being a robot, devoid of passion and spirit, is obviously the way forward for the modern-day footballer.

GARY NEVILLE

Why couldn't you beat a richer club? I've never seen a bag of money score a goal.

JOHAN CRUYFF

Wisey said I think too much. But I have to do all his thinking for him.

GIANFRANCO ZOLA

If a player is not interfering with play or seeking to gain an advantage, then he should be.

BILL SHANKLY

You don't have to have been a horse to be a jockey.

ARRIGO SACCHI

Most kids dream of scoring the perfect goal. I've always dreamed of stopping it.

IKER CASILLAS

Need a rest? If I need a rest I'll sleep on the team bus on the way to the game.

NIGEL DE JONG

You play football with your head, your legs are there to help you.

JOHAN CRUYFF

Our squad looks good on paper. But paper teams win paper cups.

HOWARD WILKINSON

Some people tell me that we professional players are soccer slaves. Well, if this is slavery, give me a life sentence.

BOBBY CHARLTON

We aspire to be an annoying team.

DIEGO SIMEONE

We usually say that you cannot become a legend before death. But I am a living legend.

ZLATAN IBRAHIMOVIC

When you see Damien [Duff] coming out of the shower, you'd never believe he's a professional footballer.

DIDIER DROGBA

When I lost a match I broke down in frustration. Today players lose, take a selfie and put it on the Internet. They make me sick.

GENNARO GATTUSO

Whether dribbling or sprinting, Ryan can leave the best defenders with twisted blood.
SIR ALEX FERGUSON

You train dogs. I like to educate players.
BRENDAN RODGERS

When you're walking onto a bus and trying to get there before the person in front of you, that's a different level of competition to playing in front of 80,000 people.
GRAEME LE SAUX

We'll be the first team to play on Mars!
MALCOLM ALLISON

White socks look brighter and good teams wear them. I tried it during the season and we played some good stuff. You feel better and the players wanted it.

RUUD GULLIT

We grow our players at this club, we don't have a greenhouse in the back because we can't afford it, we're more of a microwave club.

AIDY BOOTHROYD

You are pushed to behave differently here, you don't really have a choice. If you cheat you have no chance of being admired. Even your own supporters will dislike you. So what do you do? Well, the way is not to be stupid, but not to cheat either. If there is a foul, you have to fall. I call it 'helping the referee to make a decision'. That's not cheating.

JOSE MOURINHO

Are you sure?

If you look at the last ten games and you turn the league table upside down, we wouldn't be far off top six.

STEPHEN HUNT

Aston Villa are seventh in the League – that's
almost as high as you can get without being
one of the top six.

IAN PAYNE

I wouldn't be bothered if we lost every game as
long as we won the league.

MARK VIDUKA

Ian Rush, deadly ten times out of ten, but that
wasn't one of them.

PETER JONES

Even if there is one game to go and we are 12
points behind, we'll still believe.

JOE HART

He was on the six- yard line, just two yards
away from the goal.

PAT NEVIN

It looks like a one man show here, although there are two men involved.

JOHN MOTSON

It looks like they'll be playing 4-4-1-2.
MARK LAWRENSON

It was six of a half and one dozen of the other.
DANNY HIGGINBOTHAM

I can't promise anything, but I promise 100 per cent.

PAUL POWER

Our keeper only had one save to make but we lost 4-0.

CRAIG BROWN

Most managers would give their right arm for a
European Cup, and Bob Paisley had three!

MANISH BHASIN

There's going to be four or five teams battling
for the top six spots.

CHRIS WADDLE

There's such a fine line between defeat and
losing.

GARY NEWBON

They lack the cherry on the cake to unlock the
door.

PHIL NEVILLE

I couldn't settle in Italy – it was like living in a
foreign country.

IAN RUSH

You cant play with a one armed goalkeeper...
not at this level.

KEVIN KEEGAN

Being given chances and not taking them. That's
what life is all about.

RON GREENWOOD

I'm going to make a prediction... It could go
either way.

RON ATKINSON

In the papers this morning, 'Police closing in on
Ian Holloway.' Sorry... it's 'Palace closing in on
Ian Holloway.'

ALAN BRAZIL

It's great to get that duck off my back.

GARY CAHILL

It's end-to-end stuff, but from side to side.

TREVOR BROOKING

John Arne Riise was deservedly blown up for that foul.

ALAN GREEN

We had a word with him about diving and since then the lad's come on leaps and bounds.

BILLY DODDS

We have to be careful not to let our game not be the game we know it should be.

PAUL INCE

We have to roll up our sleeves and get our knees dirty.

HOWARD WILKINSON

My legs sort of disappeared from nowhere.

CHRIS WADDLE

Phil Dowd checks his whistle and blows his watch.

ALAN GREEN

The Newcastle back three, back four, back five have been at sixes and sevens.

BARRY VENISON

There is no precedent for what Suarez did, other than he's done it before.

DANNY MILLS

What I said to them at half-time would be unprintable on the radio.

GERRY FRANCIS

There's a rat in the camp throwing a spanner in the works.

CHRIS CATTLIN

Winning isn't the end of the world.
DAVID PLEAT

Yeading was a potential banana blip for Newcastle.
SIR BOBBY ROBSON

You either win or you lose. There's no in between.
TERRY VENABLES

I took a whack on my left ankle, but something told me it was my right.
LEE HENDRIE

One accusation you can't throw at me is that
I've always done my best.

ALAN SHEARER

He's got his hands on his knees and holds his
head in despair.

DAVID COLEMAN

I once remember the old Bayern Munich manager
taking a two-hour session for 90 minutes.

DAN WALKER

We just ran out of legs.

DAVID PLEAT

I never make predictions and I never will.

PAUL GASCOIGNE

We managed to wrong a few rights.

KEVIN KEEGAN

As a striker, you are either in a purple patch or struggling. At the moment, I'm somewhere in between.

BOB TAYLOR

As one door closes, another one shuts.
HOWARD WILKINSON

Wimbledon are putting balls into the blender.
RODNEY MARSH

At one point of the match we felt like we were at the edge of a cliff, but we managed to do the right thing and stepped forward.
JOAO PINTO

At the end of the day, the Arsenal fans demand that we put eleven players on the pitch.
DON HOWE

Barcelona have promised their fans they will quite literally play out of their skins tonight.

CLIVE TYLDESLEY

Beckenbauer really has gambled all his eggs.
RON ATKINSON

For those of you watching in black and white, Spurs are in the all yellow strip.
JOHN MOTSON

I'm not too sure how much you get for winning the Champions League, but it's definitely 10 million euros.
DAVID PLEAT

For Wigan, this game is a cup final for them.
IAN WRIGHT, AT THE ACTUAL 2013 FA CUP FINAL

Frank Lampard has still got the same legs he had five years ago.

RAY WILKINS

Glenn [Hoddle] is putting his head in the frying pan.

OSSIE ARDILES

You're always going to be struggling if you haven't got a left foot.

TREVOR BROOKING

I can see the carrot at the end of the tunnel.

STUART PEARCE

I don't believe in superstitions. I just do certain things because I'm scared in case something will happen if I don't do them.

MICHAEL OWEN

I think in international football you have to be able to handle the ball.

GLEN HODDLE

One point from an away game is no longer considered a victory.

PETTER RUDI

I was feeling as sick as the proverbial donkey.

MICK MCCARTHY

If you cut me in half, I'm a footballer.

MICHAEL OWEN

I was surprised, but I always say nothing surprises me in football.

LES FERDINAND

I was watching the Blackburn game on TV on Sunday when it flashed on the screen that George Ndah had scored in the first minute at Birmingham. My first reaction was to ring him up, then I remembered he was out there playing.

ADE AKINBIYI

I will never forget my first game for England at the World Cup. It was against Turkey... No, I mean Tunisia.

DAVID SEAMAN

I would not say David Ginola is the best left winger in the Premiership, but there are none better.

RON ATKINSON

I wouldn't touch Chimbonda with a barn door.

ALAN BRAZIL

I'd been ill and hadn't trained for a week, and
I'd been out of the team for three weeks before
that, so I wasn't sharp. I got cramp before half-
time as well. But I'm not one to make excuses.

CLINTON MORRISON

I'd like to play for an Italian club, like Barcelona.
MARK DRAPER

If you closed your eyes, you couldn't tell the
difference between the two sides.
PHIL BROWN

I'd love to be a mole on the wall in the
Liverpool dressing room at half time.
KEVIN KEEGAN

I'm not a believer in luck, but I do believe you
need it.
ALAN BALL

I've been consistent in patches this season.

THEO WALCOTT

I've got other irons in the fire but I'm keeping them close to my chest.

JOHN BOND

Ian Rush unleashed his left foot and it hit the back of the net.

MIKE ENGLAND

If they think they can play with two fingers up their nose and a lit cigar, it is not possible.

RUUD GULLIT

If Glenn Hoddle had been any other nationality, he would have had 70 or 80 caps for England.

JOHN BARNES

Sometimes
2 + 2 = 5

It's real end to end stuff, but
unfortunately it's all up at Forest's end.

CHRIS KAMARA

If you don't believe you can win, there is no point in getting out of bed at the end of the day.

NEVILLE SOUTHALL

I'm not saying we shouldn't have a foreign manager, but I think he should definitely be English.

PAUL MERSON

I'm still wondering if that goal was down to luck or good fortune.

MARK LAWRENSON

It flew towards the roof of the net like a Wurlitzer.

GEORGE HAMILTON

It looks tough for Palace when you see some of the results they've got coming up.

SHAUN DERRY

It seems that they're playing with one leg tied together.

KENNY SANSOM

It was a good match which could have gone either way and very nearly did.

JIM SHERWIN

It's a huge honour to wear number 7 at Liverpool. I think about the legends; Dalglish, Keegan and that Australian guy.

LUIS SUAREZ CAN'T REMEMBER HARRY KEWELL

It's a lance that had to be boiled.

JOHN TERRY

It was like déjà vu all over again.

SHAKA HISLOP

It's a case of putting all our eggs into the next ninety minutes.

PHIL NEAL

Martin O'Neill standing hands on his hips, stroking his chin.

MIKE INGHAM

Matches don't come any bigger than FA Cup quarter-finals.

NEIL WARNOCK

Maths is totally done differently to what I was teached when I was at school.

DAVID BECKHAM

It's not always plain sailing, especially when you're flying.

BRENDAN RODGERS

It's one of the greatest goals ever, but I'm surprised that people are talking about it being the goal of the season.

ANDY GRAY

It's slightly alarming the way Manchester United decapitated against Stuttgart.

MARK LAWRENSON

It's the end of season curtain raiser.

PETER WITHE

Mark Hughes. Sparky by name, Sparky by nature. The same can be said of Brian McClair.

BRIAN MOORE

It's thrown a spanner in the fire.

BOBBY GOULD

It's a cup final, and the one that wins it goes through.

JIMMY HILL

Mario Balotelli is like Marmite, you either love him or hate him. Me, I'm in between.

JOE ROYLE

Mark Hughes crossed every 'i' and dotted every 't'.

ROBBIE SAVAGE

Marseille needed to score first, and that never looked likely once Liverpool had taken the lead.

DAVID PLEAT

The one thing I didn't expect is the way we didn't play.

GEORGE GRAHAM

Joe Hart made a few mistakes around Christmas time and got crucified for them.
JOE CORRIGAN

Kevin Keegan has now tasted the other side of the fence.
DAVE MERRINGTON

Kevin Keegan said if he had a blank sheet of paper, five names would be on it.
ALVIN MARTIN

Manchester United have hit the ground running – albeit with a 3-0 defeat.
BOB WILSON

Klinsmann has taken to English football like a duck out of water.

GERRY FRANCIS

I can't even remember when the Seventies was.
ROBBIE KEANE

Lampard as usual arrived in the nick of time, but it wasn't quite soon enough.

ALAN PARRY

Lampard picks his head up and knocks it out to the wing.

ALAN SHEARER

Manchester United are looking to Frank Stapleton to pull some magic out of the fire.

JIMMY HILL

Leeds is a great club and it's been my home for years, even though I live in Middlesbrough.

JONATHAN WOODGATE

Liverpool have come out with all guns flying.
DENNIS TUEART

Look at the fans behind the goal. Nobody's appealing for a Villa penalty. Okay, they're QPR fans, but...

RAY WILKINS

Let them speak...

It's a long time since I've seen a player who you feel would kick his granny to win, and that's lovely – though not for the granny.

GLENN ROEDER

It wasn't the hand of God. It was the hand of a rascal. God had nothing to do with it.

SIR BOBBY ROBSON ON MARADONA'S
INFAMOUS GOAL

It's about time us managers had a fight. I wouldn't be daft enough to have a go at Sam Allardyce but me and Bryan Robson would be decent. I'd have to kill him or he'd keep coming back at me!

STEVE BRUCE

It's not what Ginola does when he has the ball. It's what he doesn't do when he hasn't got it.

ANDY GRAY

Our major problem is that we don't know how to play football.

SAM ALLARDYCE

It's one of them days when you just say, 'It's one of them days'.

IAN WRIGHT

It's always great starting the season with a team photo which has a cheeky trophy in front of the squad. When I was at Aston Villa we posed with a photocopier under our feet because we were sponsored by its manufacturers. It just wasn't the same somehow.

MARTIN KEOWN

Jens changed his mind but wasn't quick enough to respond to his brain.

ARSENE WENGER

I like to think that, apart from being a bit of a butcher, I've something else to offer.

RON HARRIS

Mourinho is the funniest thing to come out of London since Del Boy and Rodney.

JAMIE CARRAGHER

My fondest memory of Mark Hughes is his passport picture, which was a Panini sticker of himself.

MICHAEL DUBERRY

If you pay them the wages they'll come. We all kid ourselves: 'I've wanted to play for Tottenham since I was two, I had pictures of Jimmy Greaves on my wall'. It's a load of bull. Here's £80,000 a week. Lovely jubbly.

HARRY REDKNAPP

My mother thinks I am the best. And I was raised to always believe what my mother tells me.

DIEGO MARADONA

Obviously there's a language barrier at Chelsea. The majority of the lads speak Italian, but there's a few who don't.

DENNIS WISE

One reason he's improved so much is he's stopped messing about with his barnet.
HARRY REDKNAPP ON GARETH BALE

The news from Guadalajara where the temperature is 96°, is that Falcao is warming up.
BRIAN MOORE

Our goalscoring is like ketchup, you never now how much is going to come out of the bottle.
TROND SOLLIED

They say Rome wasn't built in a day, but I wasn't on that particular job.
BRIAN CLOUGH

In the tunnel, I say to David Elleray, 'You might
as well book me now and get it over with'. He
takes it pretty well but he still books me.

ROY KEANE

People used to say that if I'd shot John Lennon,
he'd still be alive today.

GARY BIRTLES

Peter Schmeichel reckons the present Man
United side [in 1999] would beat the 1968
European Cup winners. He's got a point,
because we're all over 50 now.

NOBBY STILES

Sadly, I have been unable to persuade FIFA,
UEFA and the Premier League to allow me to
use 12 players in every game.

RAFA BENITEZ

Scottish cup sponsor Willie Haughey: He's made his millions out of refrigeration. You could say he's a fridge magnate.

JEFF STELLING

The boys' performance was so good that I've run out of expletives to describe it.
MICKY MELLON

Someone asked me last week if I miss the Villa. I said, 'No, I live in one.'
DAVID PLATT ENJOYING LIFE IN ITALY

Sometimes you look in a field and see a cow. You think it's a better cow than the one you see in your field. It never really works out that way.
SIR ALEX FERGUSON

Suker - first touch like a camel.
RON ATKINSON

That boy throws a ball further than I go on holiday.

RON ATKINSON ON TRANMERE'S
DAVE CHALLINOR

The Dutch look like a huge jar of marmalade.
BARRY DAVIES

The match will be shown on Match of the Day this evening. If you don't want to know the result, look away now as we show you Tony Adams lifting the trophy for Arsenal.
– STEVE RIDER

This is a difficult division. Apart from the top four, it's dog eat dog, and we have just eaten one of the dogs.
KEVIN KEEGAN

The keeper was coming out in instalments.

JOE ROYLE

The lifestyle is much the same – bad clothing,
bad food – so we don't expect too much.
ALFIE HAALAND, ON NORWAY AND ENGLAND

The little lad jumped like a salmon and tackled
like a ferret.
SIR BOBBY ROBSON

Their team is like a bad haircut, long up front
but short at the back.
ROBBIE EARLE

The manager said at half-time if I got six, he
might give me a Mars bar. I'll have to go out
and buy my own now, won't I?
ALAN SHEARER ONLY SCORED 5 THAT DAY

What's it like being in Bethlehem, the place where Christmas began? I suppose it's like seeing Ian Wright at Arsenal.

SIMON FANSHAWE

The only thing I have in common with George Best is that we come from the same place, played for the same club and were discovered by the same man.

NORMAN WHITESIDE

The press in England make from a little mosquito a big elephant.

RUUD GULLIT

The sooner [Steve] McMahon returns the better. I have been so stiff recently on the morning after matches that I thought rigor mortis had set in.

PETER REID

The trouble with you, son, is that your brains are all in your head.

BILL SHANKLY

There is no chance I would ever consider having all my hair cut off. My hair is my life. It's so important to me. If you cut off my hair, it is like cutting out my heart or cutting off my legs. I would cry for days and days.

ANDERSON

There was never a relationship to begin with between me and Glenn Hoddle but you could say it deteriorated in that last year. Even the tea lady would have got a game before me.

ROBERT FLECK

It all makes perfect sense

There was nothing wrong with his timing.
He was just a bit late.

MARK BRIGHT

The ref was vertically 15 yards away.

KEVIN KEEGAN

The Scots have really got their hands cut out
tonight.

TREVOR FRANCIS

The sky is the limit for Jamie Paterson as long as
we keep his feet on the ground.

ANDY REID

There's a little triangle - five left-footed players.

RON ATKINSON

The tackles are coming in thick and thin.

ALAN BRAZIL

The team must try to get their ship back on the road.

RAY WILKINS

The tide is very much in our court now.
KEVIN KEEGAN

The underdogs will start favourites for this match.
CRAIG BROWN

There are a lot of tired legs wearing Tottenham shirts.
ANDY GRAY

The Uruguayans are losing no time in making a meal around the referee.
MIKE INGHAM

The way forwards is backwards.

DAVE SEXTON

The world is my lobster.

KEITH O'NEILL

There'll be no siestas in Madrid tonight.

KEVIN KEEGAN

Not to win is guttering.

MARK NOBLE

There are so many teams now down at the bottom of the Third Division. The FA really has to do something about it.

PETER LORIMER

There is great harmonium in the dressing room.

SIR ALF RAMSEY

There's Bergkamp standing on the halfway line, with his hands on his hips, flailing his arms about.

JOHN SCALES

There's enough British managers out there, come on... off the top of my head, why not Thierry Henry?

PAUL MERSON

There's no in between – you're either good or bad. We were in between.

GARY LINEKER

There's one that hasn't been cancelled because of the Arctic conditions – it's been cancelled because of a frozen pitch.

BOB WILSON

There's no point looking back on it but we'll reflect on it.

MARK HUGHES

There's no such thing as a must-win game, and this is one of them.

ALAN WRIGHT

There's no one to blame – they're just individual mistakes.

DAVID BECKHAM

They've one man to thank for that goal, Alan Shearer. And they've also got to thank referee Alan Wilkie.

CHRIS KAMARA

There's Thierry Henry, exploding like the French train that he is.

DAVID PLEAT

There's only one person gets you sacked and that's the fans.

PAUL MERSON

There's only one possibility: win, draw, or lose.
FRANZ BECKENBAUER

These managers all know their onions and cut their cloth accordingly.
MARK LAWRENSON

Think of a number between 10 and 11.
RON ATKINSON

They always say that you never learn unless you lose or make a bad mistake in a game. So I learned a lot from last season...I owe Kevin Keegan a lot.
SHAUN WRIGHT PHILLIPS

They are playing above the ground.

RON ATKINSON

They can crumble as easily as ice cream in this heat.

SAMMY NELSON

They didn't change positions. They just moved the players around.

TERRY VENABLES

This performance today shows that other teams are going to have to score more goals than us if they want to beat us.

DARREN BENT

They gave the Serbian FA a poultry fine.

ALAN BRAZIL

They were still in the dressing room when they came out for the second half.

GLENN HODDLE

They're the second best team in the world, and there's no higher praise than that.

KEVIN KEEGAN

Three words... Yaya Toure.

ANDY GRAY

They've forced them into a lot of unforced errors.

STEVE CLARIDGE

They've picked their heads up off the ground, and they now have a lot to carry on their shoulders.

RON ATKINSON

Hmmm!

In some ways, cramp is worse than having a broken leg.

KEVIN KEEGAN

Kilbane's like a one-eyed cat in a fish shop - he doesn't know what to do or where to go.

MARK LAWRENSON

Managers are like fish ... after a while they start to smell.

GIOVANNI TRAPATTONI

This is a real cat and carrot situation.

DAVID PLEAT

So different from the scenes in 1872, at the cup final none of us can remember.

JOHN MOTSON

Football's like a big market place, and people go to the market every day to buy their vegetables.

BOBBY ROBSON

When you're dealing with someone who only has a pair of underpants on, if you take his underpants off he has nothing left. He's naked. You're better off trying to find him a pair of trousers to complement him rather than change him.

ARSENE WENGER

You can't switch the lights on every time and we didn't smell that one coming. The car was in neutral and we couldn't put it in drive.

GLENN HODDLE

I am not superstitious. It brings bad luck.

RAYMOND DOMENECH

You get bunches of players like you do bananas, though that is a bad comparison.

KEVIN KEEGAN

Ziege hits it high for Heskey, who isn't playing.

ALAN GREEN

Apparently when you head a football, you lose brain cells, but it doesn't bother me... I'm a horse. No one's proved it yet have they?

DAVID MAY

Arsenal haven't won anything for three years, so they're used to success.

GLENN HODDLE

Every dog has its day, and today is woof day! Today I just want to bark!

IAN HOLLOWAY

Football managers are like a parachutist. At times it doesn't open. Here, it is an umbrella. You understand, Mary Poppins.

CLAUDIO RANIERI

I will never find any difference between Pele's pass to Carlos Alberto in the final of the 1970 World Cup and the poetry of young Rimbaud.

ERIC CANTONA

We can't behave like crocodiles and cry over spilled milk and broken eggs.
GIOVANNI TRAPATTONI

The candle is still very much in the melting pot.
ALAN MCINALLY

I'm not convinced that Scotland will play a typically English game.
GARETH SOUTHGATE

I've lost count of the times I've played in that fixture. Each one was a memorable occasion.
TREVOR STEVEN

If Chelsea drop points, the cat's out in the open.
And you know what cats are like – sometimes
they don't come home.

SIR ALEX FERGUSON

If Dennis Bergkamp was in Star Trek, he'd be the
best player in whatever solar system they were
in.

IAN WRIGHT

If it is the case that you need just a first 11 and
three or four more players, then why did
Christopher Columbus sail to India to discover
America?

CLAUDIO RANIERI

If you hire people who are smarter than you,
maybe you are showing that you are a little bit
smarter than them.

HOWARD WILKINSON

If you were to take an aerial photo of Basel today, it would look like a piece of toast with marmalade on it.

CLIVE TYLDESLEY

If, as some people think, there is such a thing as reincarnation, I'd love to come back as an eagle. I love the way eagles move, the way they soar, the way they gaze.

ERIC CANTONA

In Spain the great forwards, like the best perfumes of the world, come in a small container.

JORGE VALDANO

International football is one clog further up the football ladder.

GLEN HODDLE

It was handbags at half-mast, really.

ALAN PARDEW

It's like having a blanket that is too small for the bed. You pull the blanket up to keep your chest warm and your feet stick out. I cannot buy a bigger blanket because the supermarket is closed, but the blanket is made of cashmere.

JOSE MOURINHO

Madrid are like a rabbit dazed in the headlights of a car, except this rabbit has a suit of armour, in the shape of two precious away goals.

GEORGE HAMILTON

It's understandable that people are keeping one eye on the pot and another up the chimney.

KEVIN KEEGAN

I don't know if you know, but with the football kit today there are no pockets. Nobody can put their hands in their pockets.

AVRAM GRANT

Just one minute of overtime, so you can put the eggs on now if you like.

JOHN MOTSON

Now they have got an extra yard of doubtness in their minds.

CHRIS KAMARA

My biggest mentor is myself, because I've had to study, so that's been my biggest influence.

BRENDAN RODGERS

Nicolas Anelka left Arsenal for £23million and they built a training ground on him.

KEVIN KEEGAN

No regrets. None at all. My only regret is that we went out on penalties. That's my only regret but no, no regrets.

MICK MCCARTHY

None of the player are wearing earrings. Kjeldberg, with his contact lenses is the closest we can get.

JOHN MOTSON

Not the first half you might have expected, even though the score might suggest that it was.

JOHN MOTSON

The circus came to town but the lions and tigers didn't turn up.

KEVIN KEEGAN

Romania are more Portuguese than German.

BARRY VENISON

Really?

When I'm out on the pitch it's the closest thing to being back in a dressing room.

STEVE BAINES

Well, I can play in the centre, on the right and occasionally on the left side.

DAVID BECKHAM, WHEN ASKED IF HE WAS
'VOLATILE'

Well, I've seen some tackles, Jonathan, but that was the ultimatum!

ALAN MULLERY

What do you think of Manchester United's three Rs; Rooney, Ronaldo and van Nistelroy?

ROB MCCAFFREY

Where do you get an experienced player like him with a left foot and a head?

BOBBY ROBSON

Who'll win the league? It's a toss of a coin between three of them.

MATT LE TISSIER

Whoever wins today will win the championship no matter who wins.

DENIS LAW

Wigan Athletic are certain to be promoted barring a mathematical tragedy.

TONY GUBBA

Winning doesn't really matter as long as you win.

VINNY JONES

The 33 or 34-year-olds will be 36 or 37 by the time the next World Cup comes around, if they're not careful.

KEVIN KEEGAN

With hindsight, it's easy to look at it with hindsight.

GLENN HODDLE

With the very last kick of the game, Bobby McDonald scored with a header.

ALAN PARRY

Yes, Woodcock would have scored but his shot was just too perfect.

RON ATKINSON

You can never beat Alex Ferguson and when you do, you come off second best.

STEVE MCCLAREN

You're on your own out there with ten mates.

MICHAEL OWEN

You can't say my team aren't winners. They've proved that by finishing fourth, third and second in the past three seasons.

GERARD HOULLIER

You can't really grumble at the red card but it's very harsh.

MICHAEL OWEN

When David Beckham leaves the game, it will take a very special player to come in and carry the mantelpiece.

SOPHIE NICOLAU

You could visibly hear the strain in his voice.

MIKE PARRY

You don't need balls to play in a cup final.

STEVE CLARIDGE

You don't want to be giving away free kicks in the penalty area.

RON ATKINSON

You don't score 64 goals in 86 games at the highest level without being able to score goals.

ALAN GREEN

You feel if Chile could just organise, they could hammer Austria nil-nil.

JON CHAMPION

You half fancied that to go in as it was rising and dipping at the same time.

RON ATKINSON

You don't get two chances at this level - or any other level for that matter.

KEVIN KEEGAN

You need 15 players of that elk and then keep them together.

BOBBY GOULD

You need to take your rose-scented glasses off.

ROBBIE SAVAGE

You weigh up the pros and cons and try to put them into chronological order.

DAVE BASSETT

You'd have put your kitchen sink on Hernandez to score there.

MICK MARTIN

You usually like to play promoted sides around Christmas. They have got two lungs at the moment.

PAUL MERSON

You're either very good or very bad. There's no in between. We were in between.

GARY LINEKER

You're not just getting international football, you're getting world football.

KEVIN KEEGAN

You can only do as well as what you have done.
BRYAN ROBSON

This team never lose games – they just run out of time occasionally.

STEVE MCCLAREN

You're not sure if the ball is going to bounce up or down.

FRANK STAPLETON

When they first installed all-seater stadiums, everyone predicted that the fans wouldn't stand for it.

GEORGE BEST

Printed in Great Britain
by Amazon